MAR 2 4 2016

D1252329

TOTALLY GROSS HISTORY™

THE TOTALLY GROSS HISTORY OF
ANCIENT GREECE

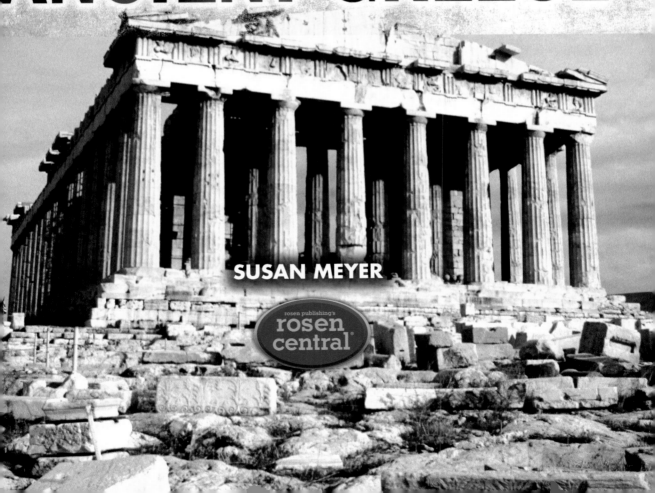

SUSAN MEYER

rosen publishing's
rosen
central®

Published in 2016 by The Rosen Publishing Group, Inc.
29 East 21st Street, New York, NY 10010

Copyright © 2016 by The Rosen Publishing Group, Inc.

First Edition

All rights reserved. No part of this book may be reproduced in any form without permission in writing from the publisher, except by a reviewer.

Library of Congress Cataloging-in-Publication Data

Meyer, Susan.
The totally gross history of ancient Greece / Susan Meyer. — First edition.
    pages cm — (Totally gross history)
Includes bibliographical references and index.
ISBN 978-1-4994-3750-8 (library bound) — ISBN 978-1-4994-3748-5 (pbk.) — ISBN 978-1-4994-3749-2 (6-pack)
1. Greece—Civilization—To 146 B.C.—Juvenile literature. I. Title.
DF78.M44 2016
938--dc23

2015022269

Manufactured in the United States of America

CONTENTS

INTRODUCTION

The civilization of ancient Greece brought many astounding innovations and ideas that still influence the world today. Ancient Greece is generally considered to be the time period from the eighth to sixth centuries BCE through the Classical Period (500–323 BCE) and Hellenistic Period (323–146 BCE). It didn't end until the Greek civilization fell to the Romans in 146 BCE.

In that large span of time, the Greeks had many great new ideas. They invented a form of government called democracy, which is the foundation for the United States government. The Greeks invented philosophy as we understand it today. Greek philosophers like Plato and Aristotle provide the cornerstone for modern philosophy. The Greeks also wrote some of the earliest and most detailed histories, which is why people today are able to know so much about their lives. Greek writers and storytellers contributed wonderful literature and poetry that is still read today. Some of history's earliest-known dramatic productions were put on in the city of Athens in ancient Greece. The Greeks honed the art of drama, dividing it into the genres of tragedy and comedy. Fans of biennial athletics can also thank the Greeks for starting the Olympic Games.

Beyond these ideas, the Greeks produced many inventions. They created detailed columned architecture and sculptures, some so strong that they still stand today. A Greek mathematician named Euclid created the foundations of geometry.

The ancient Greeks, including philosphers Plato and Aristotle, advanced Western civilization in remarkable ways. But for all its sophistication, ancient Greece could be really gross.

And a Greek doctor named Hippocrates created the idea of modern medicine that says that observing patients is the way to find cures for them. The Greeks also created valuable technologies like the water mill. The list of Greek accomplishments goes on and on.

But this book is not about all the world-changing ideas credited to the civilization of ancient Greece. No, this book is about how the Greeks lived their lives and, in particular, the rather disgusting aspects of life in ancient Greece. Despite their theater, literature, evolved thinking, the Greeks didn't have indoor plumbing. They also had some curious eating habits and ate many things modern eaters might turn their noses up at. They had some wacky ideas about medicine. Even Hippocrates, known as the Father of Medicine, had a revolting way of diagnosing his patients. The Greeks could also be bloodthirsty in battle, and one Greek king in particular had a truly barbaric torture device. And for all the stories and literature they provided, perhaps the most memorable are the Greek myths, which include some pretty dark and disturbing tales.

All in all, the culture of ancient Greece was pretty amazing, but it was also pretty gross. This resource will set aside the many awe-inspiring accomplishments of the ancient Greeks and instead dive into the most nose-wrinkling and stomach-churning facts and stories about what life was like in ancient Greece.

CHAPTER ONE

HIDEOUS HYGIENE

These days indoor plumbing is something most people in the Western world take for granted. Toilets flush waste away to modern waste treatment facilities. Clean water for drinking and showering is also available with just the turn of a faucet. Daily life in ancient Greece was not quite so simple or so hygienic.

SEWAGE IN THE STREETS

Greeks had a much more public society than many cultures of the modern world. Ancient Greeks would bathe in groups in big rooms in what were called public baths. Public baths also had public toilets. These were a little different from the public toilets we have today. The public toilets of ancient Greece didn't have stalls for privacy of any kind. Instead they had just a series of holes lined up where people would use the facilities side by side. Modesty wasn't as important to the ancient Greeks.

Many people would happily urinate or defecate right in the middle of the street as well. After all, there weren't any laws against it, and it was convenient. In the home, people sometimes had chamber pots. A chamber pot is basically a bucket where the Greeks could do their business, particularly at night. In the morning, the chamber pot would be emptied, often directly into the street.

So where did all this sewage go? Well, that's just it. It didn't go anywhere. There were no pipes and plumbing to take away waste, so instead it built up. In larger cities, like Athens, where

Aqueducts enabled the ancient Greeks to bring clean drinking water to the public fountains of their cities. Many of these structures still exist today.

many people lived together, this quickly became a problem. In addition to smelling foul, it also made the drinking water unsafe. The Greeks soon had to invent an early method of plumbing. This did not drain away the waste, however, but instead piped in drinkable water from cleaner places. Piping in water from other cities might not seem like a big deal now, but at the time it was a huge feat of engineering. Sometimes the greatest technological advances are the result of gross necessity.

Without toilets, it's not surprising that the Greeks didn't have toilet paper either. Instead they used sponges attached to the ends of sticks. They also used small stones called *pessoi* to wipe. Archaeologists first believed these pebbles were used for some kind of game. Then they noticed that they kept finding the stones in the remains of ancient Greek toilets and realized pessoi had another, very important purpose. These small stones were apparently effective for wiping, but modern scientists believe they might have led to some long-term irritation.

It is thought by some archaeologists that the first pessoi might have originated from

This piece of ancient pottery was the chamber pot of a Greek child. Given enough time, even a toilet can help tell the story of past civilizations.

ostaka. Ostaka were shards of pottery that people would write their enemies' names on to vote them out of town. The word "ostracize" that we use today, meaning to banish or shun someone, comes from the Greeks' use of ostaka. Using ostaka with one's enemy's name to wipe oneself after going to the bathroom would be an extra fitting revenge on that enemy. The Greeks were nothing if not resourceful.

THE EARLIEST TOILET HUMOR

The Greeks put on some of the earliest theater productions. Many were tragedies, but some were comedies. One of the most famous comic playwrights from ancient Greece was named Aristophanes. He wrote many plays, including one in 421 BCE called *Peace*. In it, the main character Trygaeus makes some of the earliest bathroom humor at the expense of a man trying to sell him a piece of armor.

Trygaeus does not want to pay the seller for the piece of armor and says it is only good enough for him to relieve himself in. The seller gets very angry, and then Trygaeus takes it one step further. In response to the seller's protests, Trygaeus says:

Trygaeus [placing the armor on the ground like a chamber pot and squatting on it]: Like this, if you put three stones beside it. Is it not clever?

The three stones he is referring to are the pessoi that would be used to wipe instead of toilet paper. According to the *British Medical Journal*, it was a common Greek saying that three pessoi were the appropriate amount for wiping and any more than that would be wasteful.

KEEPING CLEAN

All that sewage in their cities didn't mean that the ancient Greeks did not try to stay clean. The Greek doctor Hippocrates recommended daily bathing and massaging oils on the body for good health. Most Greeks really enjoyed bathing. In fact, they found it so relaxing that they made a pastime out of it. Most personal homes did not have bathtubs, and filling one by carting buckets of water would have been a major chore. Instead, the men and women of Greece came together in the public baths to soak in the water while chatting and catching up on the news. The Greek baths were usually circular rooms with large domed roofs. The water was heated by fire beneath the floor. Alternatively, some baths heated rocks in a fire elsewhere and then placed them in the water to warm it.

The Greeks didn't have soap. Instead, to cleanse their bodies, they would cover themselves in ashes. Then they would add olive oil on top. Next they would scrape the whole grayish muck off with a curved instrument called a *stirgil*. It might not sound very

This piece of pottery shows ancient Greek women bathing. One woman holds a stirgil to scrape away dirt and grime from her body.

nice, but the ashes and oil took the dirt with it, leaving the skin squeaky clean.

Greek baths were not as intricate as the later Roman baths, but they did have some rooms with cold water and some rooms with hot water. They also had some rooms just for sweating. What could be more fun than sitting in a room and sweating with all your friends? Nevertheless, public baths like those the Greeks used still exist today in some parts of Europe, and many people happily visit saunas and spas that are a modern equivalent to the public baths of ancient Greece.

CHAPTER TWO

FOUL FOODS

The ancient Greeks ate what would be considered today a very healthy diet, but that doesn't mean that all their food would be considered tasty by modern palates. The Greeks grew much of their food and ate many fruits and vegetables. Olives and honey were also a big part of their diet. They didn't have sugar, so honey and fruit were the only way to enjoy something sweet. In addition to fruits and vegetables, they ate mostly bread and fish. They only occasionally ate other meat.

The meat they did eat was usually left over from animals that had been sacrificed to the gods. After all, why let a perfectly good sacrificial goat go to waste? When meat eating did occur, the Greeks' favorite parts of the animal were the organs. The brain and stomach were highly prized. Receiving the heart, lungs, liver, or kidney to eat was considered a great honor. Not too many people today would get quite as excited about eating the heart of a sacrificed sheep. After the organs were gone, the Greeks were not too picky about the rest of the animal. They would eat it

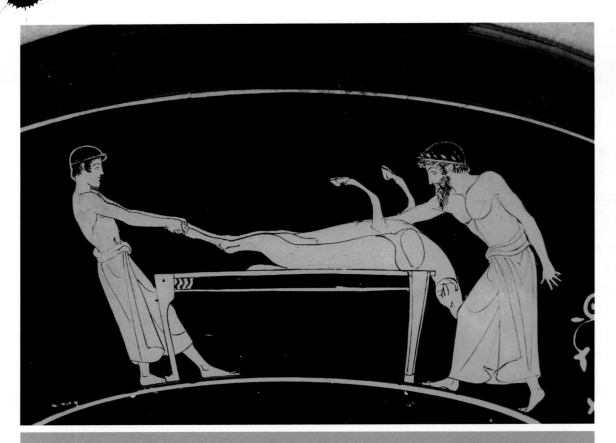

This pottery detail shows two men killing an animal for sacrifice. The ancient Greeks sacrificed animals for religious reasons, but they also ate the organs of the animal after its slaughter.

almost in entirety. They would grind the meat and blood together to make a dish called blood pudding or black pudding.

The ancient Greeks had another interesting source of protein. They would eat cicadas and grasshoppers as a protein-rich snack. The lower classes enjoyed eating grasshoppers. These insects could be purchased in the markets, but shepherds and farmers also enjoyed catching and eating them right in the

RECIPE FOR BLACK PUDDING

Black pudding is a sausage made by thickening pig's blood and molding it by stuffing it into the intestines, stomach, or bladder of an animal. This tasty treat is said to have been invented by a Greek cook named Aphtonite. The oldest surviving recipe for black pudding comes from a Roman cookbook called *De Re Coquinaria*, which translates to "The Art of Cooking." It is edited by Apicius.

In this recipe, instead of using grain to thicken the blood, chopped-up egg yolks are substituted. These are mixed with pine nuts, leeks, and onions for flavor. Then the mixture is stuffed into lengths of intestines. The stuffed casings are then cooked in broth or wine. Next time you find yourself with some pig's blood lying around, you'll know you're just a few steps away from this ancient Greek delight.

field. Cicadas, on the other hand, were preferred by upper-class Greeks. The famous philosopher Aristotle even discusses in his writings the best time of year to harvest cicadas. He said the tastiest cicadas are the ones that are not quite fully grown. He also said the females taste better when they are full of eggs.

Grasshoppers and cicadas are actually still commonly eaten in many parts of the world. This photo shows vendors in the country of Yemen selling fried grasshoppers.

Rich men and women in ancient Greece also ate slightly more evolved meat dishes. One delicacy was the pork from a pig that had died due to overeating. Naturally, this could take some time to occur, so this dish was saved for special occasions. Another dish was a bit like an omelet. However, instead of the peppers and ham modern chefs might use, the ancient Greeks mixed their eggs with brains and cheese. They wrapped the concoction in a fig leaf to eat it.

SPARTAN SOUP

The Spartan army had a reputation for having ferocious fighters. Their infantry would form a wall with their shields that was hard to penetrate. This formation was called a phalanx.

Sparta was a major city-state of ancient Greece. Spartans were known to be remarkably strong and brave. Spartan culture was very focused on making strong warriors. All men had to serve in the army, and they started from a very young age. Life for Spartan soldiers was no picnic, least of all because of their diet. The main meal for soldiers in Sparta was called black soup, or *melas zomos*. It was made of boiled pig's blood mixed with vinegar and salt. The vinegar is thought to have helped keep the blood from clotting while the soup was being made. The salt was added just to make it taste a little less like blood and vinegar. This hearty meal provided the Spartan army with strength.

There is a story that a man from southern Italy came to Sparta and tried black soup. After eating it, he said that he understood why Spartan soldiers were so willing to go off to battle and die. It is perhaps for the best that no detailed recipes for this particular dish have survived.

CHAPTER THREE

QUESTIONABLE MEDICINE

The Greeks are known to have made great contributions to the field of medicine. Greek doctors learned they could observe patients and discover cures for them, instead of just turning to the gods for help. They also made advances in anatomy and started to understand how the human body is put together and how different parts function. Most important, they wrote down many of their observations and findings so that future doctors could benefit from them.

One of the beliefs of doctors in ancient Greece was that people are made up of four humors. These are blood, black bile, yellow bile, and phlegm. Phlegm is basically mucus, or boogers. Bile is a fluid produced in the liver. Greek doctors believed that in order to be healthy, a person had to have the right balance of these four humors. Much good came out of this belief because the recommendation of doctors was that everything should be done in moderation. Exercise, regular bathing, and eating well were all encouraged. In all of this advice, Greek doctors were correct that these things would lead to improved health. Where they ran into trouble was their belief that if a person was sick, he or she might have too much of one of the four humors and need to have it released.

For example, they believed that if a patient had a fever, it was because he had too much blood. The cure for too much blood was to cut the patient to release some of the blood. This process is called bloodletting. Sometimes ancient Greek doctors used slimy leeches to help suck the blood from their patients. Leeches are helpful for this because they produce a natural chemical that keeps blood from clotting so that it will continue to flow. Interestingly, leeches are still sometimes still used in medicine today because of this property.

If the patient was thought to be sick because he or she had too much bile, doctors might have him or her eat a plant that acted as a laxative or one that would make the patient vomit. It was thought that this would help get the bad or excessive bile out of his or her system. With all the forced vomiting and bleeding, it's a wonder anyone went to the doctor at all.

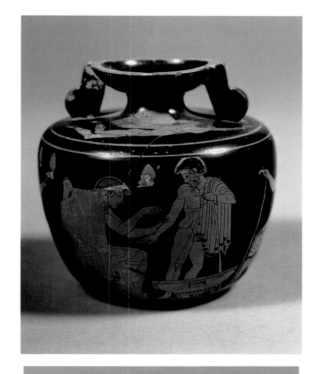

This pottery from the sixth century BCE shows a doctor practicing bloodletting. The seated doctor can be seen preparing to open the patient's arm to allow blood out.

THE DOCTORS

The most famous Greek doctor is Hippocrates. He is known as the Father of Medicine because of his many contributions to the field. He lived from 460 to 377 BCE and wrote more than fifty books on observations and ideas for how medicine should be practiced. His Hippocratic oath states that doctors should do no harm to their patients and that new doctors must swear to abide by certain ethical standards. A version of this oath is still used by doctors today.

Despite all these medical achievements, not all of this Greek doctor's "cures" exactly worked out. And many are not for the squeamish. Hippocrates observed and catalogued many of his patients' symptoms in order to find cures. He took samples of their urine, mucus, and earwax and tested them. Testing samples is perfectly acceptable today, but it is Hippocrates's method of testing them that is gross. Since he couldn't send them out to a lab for chemical analysis, as a modern doctor might do, he instead relied on his sense of taste. Yes, he actually tasted the patient's bodily secretions. You have to admit, sampling the pee and boogers of sick people is definitely going above and beyond for patients.

In ancient Greece, there were also doctors who were similar to priests. They were called the *asclepieia*. They operated healing temples, called *asclepeion*, devoted to the Greek god of medicine, Asclepius. A well-preserved asclepeion is located near the Acropolis in Athens. People would come from far away to visit the asclepeion. They would stay overnight or for many nights to be healed. The asclepeion was also just a fun place for patients

Called the Father of Medicine, Hippocrates is one of the best-known doctors from ancient Greece.

to visit, as some were not just hospital facilities but also had gymnasiums and other health and activity-related places on site. Observing patients for extended periods of time led to many medical advances. That said, not all the treatments of the asclepeion panned out.

Snakes were sometimes used in healing rituals, and it is said that they slithered around at night all over the sleeping patients. Another example of a treatment recorded as being used by the asclepieia was to allow dogs to lick the open wounds of

This illustration shows what the asclepeion might have looked like. Patients would sleep all together in one room in the temple. Some would stay at the asclepeion for many nights waiting to be healed.

a patient to increase healing. Today, doctors know much more about germs and bacteria. They know that a dog licking an open wound will certainly not make it better and will very likely make things worse.

A SMELLY "CURE"

Not everyone went to doctors for their cures. Some enterprising Greeks took controlling their diseases into their own hands. The Greek philosopher Heraclitus of Ephesus is one such case. He is said to have suffered from dropsy, which means that he had abnormal swelling and water retention.

According to many stories, Heraclitus sought to cure his dropsy by covering himself in cow manure. After applying the dung all over his body, he lay down in the sun to let the mixture dry and harden. What happens next varies in different versions of the story. In some versions, Heraclitus was completely unrecognizable covered in manure, and he was eaten by a pack of wild dogs. In other versions, there are no dogs, but the stinky covering failed to cure his dropsy. Either way, the cure was a definite dud, and Heraclitus died around 475 BCE.

DISSECTION AND VIVISECTION

The Greeks made some pretty big leaps in advancing human understanding of anatomy. Understanding how the body is put together and how it works is hugely important for medicine and surgery. One of the ways ancient Greeks gained this knowledge was through dissection. Dissection means opening up a dead body to expose the internal organs to help understand how they work. This was performed on animals like sheep and dogs. More controversially for the time, it was also performed on human corpses. In the third century BCE, two Greek doctors, Herophilus and Erasistratus, were thought to have performed some of the only regular dissections of human bodies done during ancient times. This was because for a long time afterward people were opposed to dissecting humans for moral and religious reasons. Human dissections were banned in all places in ancient Greece except for Alexandria.

Dissecting dead bodies is one thing, but it is also believed that the ancient Greeks may have practiced something even more horrifying: vivisection. Vivisection is similar to dissection, only instead of dead bodies being taken apart, bodies are taken apart while still alive. This makes it easier to see how the organs function because they are still trying to work. It is clear that vivisection on animals was practiced in ancient Greece. It is also likely that human vivisections were done. Some sources say that Herophilus may have vivisected more than six hundred prisoners during his study of anatomy.

CHAPTER FOUR

WAR AND PUNISHMENT

Daily life in ancient Greece was not always a walk in the park, but matters were even worse in wartime. Ancient Greece was divided up into many different city-states. City-states were political divisions in the Greek civilization. Each city-state had its own government and army, and each had its own distinct way of doing things. Athens is one well-known city-state. Another is Sparta. Sparta was very different from the other city-states. The people in Sparta valued bravery above all else and were very focused on the military and being ready for war. Men and women alike were trained to fight, and children entered army training at a very young age.

THE LIFE OF A SPARTAN CHILD

Because Spartans valued strength and toughness above all, they had a pretty harsh way of welcoming new Spartans into the world. When a baby was born, soldiers came to the house to bathe the new child in wine instead of water. Based on how the child responded to this unusual first bath, he or she was labeled either strong or weak. Weak babies were killed or sold into slavery. The fate of the child was determined not just by the parent, but by the government officials of the city-state. No one wanted weak new Spartans bringing them down. Some babies were left alone on a hillside to see if they could survive the elements. Babies that couldn't survive were obviously too weak.

Babies who did manage to survive were in for a pretty hard life. Children were raised by the city-state from an early age and

Spartan men spent much of their lives training for battle. This image shows what a day at the gym might have looked like for young Spartans.

left to run around in packs by themselves. They were encouraged to beat each other up and to lie and steal. They didn't bathe. They had to scrounge for scraps of food to stay alive. Through this method, the Spartans hoped to raise children who were cunning and tough in battle.

The Spartans went out of their way to raise little bullies to become strong, angry men. From the age of six or seven, boys lived in the army barracks. They stayed there until they died in battle or until they were thirty. When Spartan sons went off to battle, their mothers would tell them to return with their shields, or else on them (men who died in battle were sometimes carried back on their shields). This meant that the mother wanted to see her son return only if he was victorious or dead. A dead son was always preferable to a cowardly one.

A SPARTAN LIAR

One story of Spartan bravery begins with a young Spartan boy stealing a fox. The boy was caught for the crime but was able to hide the fox under his tunic first. While he was being questioned, the boy refused to admit that he had stolen the fox. Meanwhile, while he tried to tell a convincing-enough lie, the fox beneath his shirt ate his stomach. The boy fell over dead without ever revealing that he had stolen a fox. After all, a good Spartan was trained to show no pain.

The story comes from the writer and historian Plutarch, who wrote many books about Greece and Sparta. The story may or may not be true, but it illustrates the reputation that the Spartans had. The Spartans would have praised the boy in the story for holding out and not shedding a tear, even though it cost him his life.

SPARTAN WOMEN

Women in Sparta actually had more freedom than in other Greek city-states. In Athens, for example, women were supposed to stay at home and never be seen. (Staying at home might not seem so bad when you remember the streets were filled with sewage, but Athenian women had very few rights.) By contrast, Spartan women could go about as they pleased. They were even allowed to own and run businesses. And while the men were off fighting, the women controlled and managed the home and money.

However, for all the comparative advantages of being a woman in Sparta, their weddings weren't exactly luxurious affairs. Before getting married, Spartan brides had their heads shaved and were dressed up like men. Then they would be "kidnapped" in the night by their new husbands. The husband would sneak his bride into the barracks, and she would have to leave soon after. After this ceremony of sorts, the new husband wouldn't live with his wife until after he was allowed to leave the barracks at around age thirty. This kind of takes the shine off the honeymoon. Neither the husband nor wife would have minded too much. Another aspect of Spartan culture was that it was considered a weakness to express affection.

A SPARTAN BLOODBATH

Because the ancient Spartans focused so much on becoming warriors, they were a force to be reckoned with on the battle-field. The other city-states in Greece tried to stay on the good side of Sparta whenever possible. However, the Spartans were not invincible.

Proof of this came when the Battle of Thermopylae was fought between the Greeks and the Persians. The Persians, led by King Xeres, had begun to invade Greece in 480 BCE. Several Greek city-states banded together to help keep Greece from falling into the hands of the Persians. The Greeks decided that the Spartans should lead the Greek army because they were known to be the best warriors. In the battle in question, the Spartan warrior king Leonidas led a Greek army of only a few hundred men in an attempt to guard an important pass called Thermopylae. Unfortunately for the Greeks, they faced Persian troops of one hundred thousand men.

The Spartans and the rest of the Greeks fought bravely and with great cunning. They would pretend to retreat and then, when the Persians followed them, attack and kill many Persians in the confusion. Incredibly, after two days of fighting, the huge Persian force had been unable to defeat the Greek army, in large part because of the Spartans.

Despite their bravery, the battle would not end well for the Greeks.

At the conclusion of the Battle of Thermopylae, the Spartans were surrounded and gravely outnumbered. However, they fought bravely until the end.

A Greek traitor told the Persian army about another pass that would allow them to sneak up behind the Greeks. They would then be trapped in the Thermopylae pass—an impossible trap. Leonidas saw that he had been betrayed and was greatly outnumbered. He let the other Greeks in the army sneak away while he and his army of just three hundred Spartans remained. Knowing they faced certain defeat didn't keep him and his Spartan soldiers from fighting until the end. It is said that after the Spartans' weapons broke, they continued fighting with their hands and teeth until the Persians finally killed them.

TYRANTS AND TORTURE

Sparta may have been a pretty rough place, but it didn't contain all the cruelty in ancient Greece. Phalaris was the ruler of Acragas, a city in ancient Greece that existed in what is now the island of Sicily, off the coast of modern-day Italy. Phalaris was a tyrant. This means that he took total control of the city and ruled it with an iron fist. Phalaris was known far and wide for his cruelty. There are many stories about him told by Greek historians, some of which may not be true. One story says that he was a cannibal and that he was even known to devour babies.

Another story about Phalaris, and one that is most likely true as it appears in multiple histories of ancient Greece, is the story of his "brazen bull." Designed by a well-known Athenian bronze worker named Perilaus, the bull was an instrument used

Phalaris was the tyrannical ruler of Acragas. After commissioning Perilaus to build him a torture chamber in the image of a bull, Phalaris ordered the bronze worker to test it out.

to torture people. It was a giant hollow sculpture in the shape of a bull made entirely of bronze. Criminals or anyone else that Phalaris didn't like would be locked inside the bull. Then a fire would be lit underneath it. The victim would be roasted to death inside the bull. Phalaris even had it designed so that the screams of the victim would funnel out through the nose and make a sound like a bull. It is said that after Perilaus finished designing the bull for Phalaris that Phalaris made him get inside to try it out. Thus the inventor Perilaus was tortured to death by his own invention.

CHAPTER FIVE

MISERABLE MYTHS

The ancient Greeks maintained a rich mythology that is part of their incredible contribution to literature today. The Greeks worshipped many gods and goddesses, and great storytellers like Homer passed on their stories through oral tradition. In addition to the stories of the gods and goddesses, many myths also tell of great heroes and monsters. Not all of these stories are sunny, and many have some rather disturbing episodes. In fact, it's fair to say these stories are full of grisly murders and violent punishments. This made for some very interesting storytelling for the ancient Greeks.

HOW THE GODS CAME TO RULE

To find the first unpleasant tale, one need look no further than the Greeks' story of how the world came to be. This is outlined in a book called the *Theogony*. Before there were gods, goddesses, people, or even the Earth, there was Chaos.

Chaos created Gaea, Mother Earth, and Uranus, the ruler of the sky and heavens. Gaea and Uranus

This sculpture depicts the Titan Cronus in the process of eating one of his children. He believed that by eating them all, none of them could ever overthrow him. Unfortunately for Cronus, that turned out to be wrong.

joined together, and their children were the Titans. The Titans were powerful divine beings, similar to gods. Uranus was a cruel father, and he was eventually overthrown by one of his sons, one of the Titans named Cronus.

Cronus married his sister, another Titan, Rhea. This kind of thing happened a lot in Greek mythology, and it seldom ended well. Cronus and Rhea's children were the gods and goddesses. However, after overthrowing his own father, Cronus knew that it was prophesied that he would be overthrown by one of his sons. To stop this from happening, he took to eating his own children. Rhea was none too happy to see her children being eaten, so she saved one from Cronus's clutches and hid him away where Cronus couldn't find him. This child, Zeus, grew up and returned to Cronus disguised and bearing a poison that would make his father throw up all of Zeus's siblings. Cronus vomited up the gods and goddesses he had eaten, and together they went on to overthrow him and the other Titans and banish them to the Underworld. And that little tale of family dysfunction is how the gods and goddesses of ancient Greece came to rule over the world.

GHASTLY MYTHOLOGICAL DEATHS

Many of the Greek myths carried lessons in them and were warnings to those humans who might defy the gods. Humans who didn't respect the gods and goddesses were often punished in gruesome ways. One example is Erysichthon, who was a king of Thessaly in Greek myth. According to one myth, he chopped down the trees in a sacred forest that was guarded by

Demeter, the Greek goddess of the harvest. Demeter was angry and cursed Erysichthon with a constant hunger. No matter how much he ate, he always felt like he was starving. The king sold all his possessions and palaces for food, but it still wasn't enough. In the end, he ended up eating himself, all because he crossed a goddess.

Humans weren't the only ones who faced harsh punishments in mythology. Prometheus was one of the original Titans. He sided with Zeus during his fight against Cronus and the other Titans and was allowed to stay on Earth after the other Titans were banished. However, Prometheus didn't stay in Zeus's good graces for long. He is said to have stolen fire from Mount Olympus, where the gods lived, and given it to the humans on Earth. His punishment for this act of kindness to humanity was eternal suffering. Zeus doomed Prometheus to have his liver eaten out of him by an eagle every day for his endless life.

Prometheus's punishment for bringing fire to mankind was to lie helpless while an eagle ate away at him every day for all eternity.

Many gods and goddesses were also very jealous and punished those whom they were jealous of. Adonis was a god of love and beauty who was gored to death by a wild boar. The boar was sent by the goddess

TALKING TO THE GODS

Given how cruel the gods and goddesses could be when disrespected, it's understandable that humans would try to do whatever they could to keep from angering them. The Greeks communicated with their gods through oracles. Oracles were people specially trained to interpret messages from the gods and to help predict the future. One method oracles used for understanding their gods was called hepatoscopy.

Hepatoscopy was the practice of examining the liver of a sacrificed animal, such as a goat or sheep, in search of messages from the gods. The liver was divided up into sections that represented the different gods and goddesses. Markings on the sections were interpreted by the oracles to have different meanings. It's sort of like reading someone's palm, just a lot grosser.

Artemis, who was envious of Adonis's hunting skills. Artemis was responsible for another harsh killing. This time the target of her wrath was the hunter Actaeon. Actaeon is said to have come across Artemis in the woods when she was bathing and spied on the goddess. As punishment, she turned the hunter into a deer. Unfortunately for Actaeon, his pack of hunting dogs was still nearby. They didn't recognize their master in his new deer form and tore him to shreds.

Then there were the mythological characters who were cruel just for the fun of it. Procrustes was a son of Poseidon, the god of the oceans. Procrustes would invite houseguests to stay with him but then made them sleep in an iron bed. He wanted his guests to fit the bed perfectly, so if they were too short, he would use hammers to stretch them. If they were too tall, he chopped off their legs to make them fit. Procrustes would eventually meet his comeuppance. The hero Theseus captured Procrustes and made *him* fit into the iron bed himself. As with the story of Actaeon, there is a theme in Greek myths of the villain becoming the victim and the hunter becoming the hunted.

Many of the punishments given by the gods and goddesses were cruelly fitting. For example, the hunter Actaeon became the hunted. He was turned into a deer and killed by his own dogs.

The Greek myths are filled with many more sickening and horrifying tales. If you're looking for some fascinating reading material and you have a strong stomach, look no further than the mythology of the ancient Greeks.

The ancient Greeks produced many wonderful innovations and technologies that dramatically changed the world. But there were some aspects of their lives that cause a few raised eyebrows from modern people thousands of years later. It can be difficult to judge people who lived in such a different time and have such a different way of life from people today.

It is hard not to wonder what people thousands of years from now will make of our daily lives. Will they be disgusted by the fast food and frozen pizzas that we find delicious? Will they marvel at aspects of our lives that seem so normal, like driving pollution-producing vehicles or undergoing plastic surgery to look nicer? Only time will tell. After all, it is for future generations to decide what gross and disgusting things people will come up with next.

GLOSSARY

biennial Occurring every two years.

bloodletting Intentionally releasing blood from someone as a way of curing him or her.

city-state A political division in ancient Greece.

democracy Government in which the people elect their rulers.

dissection Taking something apart to see how it works.

dysfunction A state of being that is not normal or healthy.

hygienic Clean; free of germs.

laxative A medicine given to make someone defecate.

ostracize To shun someone from a group.

phlegm Mucus.

prophesy A prediction of the future.

secretion A fluid given off by a body.

sewage Bathroom waste.

stirgil A curved blade used for scraping dirt from the body.

tyrant A cruel ruler who abuses power.

vivisection Taking a living being apart while it is still alive.

FOR MORE INFORMATION

Acropolis Museum
Dionysiou Areopagitou 15
Athens 117 42
Greece
Website: http://www.theacropolismuseum.gr/en
The Acropolis Museum centers around the archeological site
of the acropolis in Athens. It focuses on the artifacts discovered there and what they tell us about ancient Greek life.

Athens War Museum
Rizari 2
Athens
Greece
Website: http://www.warmuseum.gr
This museum houses artifacts of the Greek military throughout its history. It includes exhibits on the early weapons
and fortification plans of the ancient Greeks.

Canadian Museum of History
100 Rue Laurier
Gatineau, QC K1A 0M8
Canada
(819) 776-7000
Website: http://www.historymuseum.ca
This museum, located in Quebec, possesses one of the largest
collections of Greek artifacts in Canada. Its website also provides helpful context and research about the ancient Greek
civilization.

Metropolitan Museum of Art
1000 Fifth Avenue
New York, NY 10028
(212) 535-7710
Website: http://www.metmuseum.org
The Metropolitan Museum of Art in New York City has a large
    collection and body of research around the Greek civilization.
    Its website also contains a detailed timeline of ancient Greece.

National Archaeological Museum of Athens
44 Patission Street
Athens
Greece
Website: http://www.namuseum.gr/wellcome-en.html
This museum is the largest archeological museum in Greece and
    one of the largest collections of Greek artifacts in the world.

WEBSITES

Because of the changing nature of Internet links, Rosen Publishing has developed an online list of websites related to the subject
of this book. This site is updated regularly. Please use this link to
access this list:

http://www.rosenlinks.com/TGH/Greece

FOR FURTHER READING

Anderson, Michael. *Ancient Greece*. New York, NY: Britannica Educational Publishing, 2012.

Bensinger, Henry. *Ancient Greek Technology*. New York, NY: Rosen Publishing Group, 2014.

Bliquez, Lawrence J. *Tools of Asclepius: Surgical Instruments in Greek and Roman Times*. Leiden, Netherlands: Brill Academic Publishers, 2014.

Bradford, Alfred. *Leonidas and the Kings of Sparta: Mightiest Warriors, Fairest Kingdom*. Santa Barbara, CA: ABC-Clio, 2011.

Caper, William. *Ancient Greece: An Interactive History Adventure*. Mankato, MN: Capstone Press, 2010.

Dalby, Andrew. *Food in the Ancient World from A to Z*. London, England: Routledge, 2013.

Garland, Robert. *Ancient Greece: Everyday Life in the Birthplace of Western Civilization*. New York, NY: Sterling Publishing, 2013.

Gifford, Clive, and Paul Cherrill. *Food and Cooking in Ancient Greece* (Cooking in World Cultures). New York, NY: PowerKids Press, 2010.

Hutchison, Godfrey. *Sparta: Unfit for Empire*. Chicago, IL: Frontline Books, 2015.

Lunge-Larsen, Lise, and Gareth Hinds. *Gifts from the Gods: Ancient Words and Wisdom from Greek and Roman Mythology*. New York, NY: Houghton Mifflin Harcourt, 2011.

MacDonald, Fiona. *You Wouldn't Want to Be a Slave in Ancient Greece!* Danbury, CT: Franklin Watts, 2013.

Nutton, Vivian. *Ancient Medicine*. London, England: Routledge, 2012.

Pearson, Anne. *DK Eyewitness Books: Ancient Greece*. New York, NY: DK Eyewitness Books, 2014.

Phillips, Martin R. *Ancient Greece*. Nanaimo, Canada: Hill Tech Ventures, 2014.

Townsend, Michael. *Amazing Greek Myths of Wonder and Blunder*. New York, NY: The Penguin Group, 2013.

Turner, Tracey, and Jamie Lenman. *Hard as Nails in Ancient Greece*. New York, NY: Crabtree Publishing, 2015.

Ward, Brian R. *The Story of Medicine*. New York, NY: Rosen Central, 2012.

BIBLIOGRAPHY

Adkins, Lesley, and Roy A. Adkins. *Handbook of Life in Ancient Greece*. New York, NY: Oxford University Press, 2005.

Apicius. *Cookery and Dining in Imperial Rome*. Translated by Joseph Dommers Vehling. Project Gutenberg. Retrieved March 10, 2015 (http://www.gutenberg.org/files/29728/29728-h/29728-h.ht).

Collins, Derek. "Mapping the Entrails: The Practice of Greek Hepatoscopy." *American Journal of Philology*, Vol. 129, No. 3, Fall 2008.

Day, Nancy. *Your Travel Guide to Ancient Greece*. Minneapolis, MN: Lerner Publishing Group, 2001.

Deary, Terry, and Martin Brown. *Horrible Histories: Groovy Greeks*. New York, NY: Scholastic Nonfiction, 2011.

Garland, Robert. *Daily Life of the Ancient Greeks*. Westport, CT: Greenwood Press, 2008.

Grmek, Mirko D., and Mireille Muellner. *Diseases in the Ancient Greek World*. Baltimore, MD: Johns Hopkins University Press, 1991.

Hamilton, Edith. *Mythology: Timeless Tales of Gods and Heroes*. Reprint. New York, NY: Grand Central Publishing, 2013.

Kipfer, Barbara Ann. *The Culinarian: A Kitchen Desk Reference*. New York, NY: Houghton Mifflin Harcourt, 2012.

Staden, H. von. "The Discovery of the Body: Human Dissection and Its Cultural Contexts in Ancient Greece." *Yale Journal of Biological Medicine*, May–June 1992.

Temkin, Owsei. *Hippocrates in a World of Pagans and Christians*. Baltimore, MD: Johns Hopkins University Press, 1991.

INDEX

ABOUT THE AUTHOR

Susan Meyer enjoys studying the civilization of ancient Greece, for both its gross and amazing achievements. She hopes to visit modern Greece one day as a continuation of her travels in parts of the former Greek Empire in Turkey. Meyer has written numerous books for Rosen Publishing. She currently lives in Austin, Texas, with her husband, Sam, and her cat, Dinah.

PHOTO CREDITS

Cover, p. 1 MyLoupe/UIG/Getty Images; p. 5 Heritage Images/Hulton Archive/Getty Images; p. 8 Hans Laubel/E+/Getty Images; p. 9 Agora Museum, Athens, Greece/Bridgeman Images; pp. 11, 14 Erich Lessing/Art Resource, NY; p. 15 Anadolu Agency/Getty Images; pp. 16, 29 Private Collection/© Look and Learn/Bridgeman Images; p. 19 DEA/G. Dagli Orti/De Agostini/Getty Images; p. 21 Stock Montage/Archive Photos/Getty Images; p. 22 Private Collection/De Agostini Picture Library/Bridgeman Images; p. 26 © Mary Evans Picture Library/Alamy; p. 31 Universal History Archive/UIG/Getty Images; p. 34 © Alex Ramsay/Alamy; p. 36 © World History Archive/Alamy; p. 38 DEA/A. De Gregorio/De Agostini/Getty Images; cover and interior pages Lukiyanova Natalia/frenta/Shutterstock.com (splatters), idea for life/Shutterstock.com, Ensuper/Shutterstock.com, ilolab/Shutterstock.com, Sfio Cracho/Shutterstock.com, Apostrophe/Shutterstock.com (textures and patterns)

Designer: Michael Moy; Editor: Christine Poolos; Photo Researcher: Nicole Baker